Travels Across America's Past

The West
Its History and People

Gare Thompson

Picture Credits

Cover (top), cover (bottom), pages 5 (top right), 6 (bottom middle), 11 (right), 19 (right), 21 (right), 24, 26 (inset), 30 (top left) Hulton-Archive/Getty Images; page 1 (bottom) Francis G. Mayer/Corbis; pages 2–3 St. Louis Art Museum; pages 4–5 (bottom) Hulton-Deutsch Collection/Corbis; pages 4 (bottom middle), 7 (bottom middle), 7 (bottom right), 18 (bottom inset), 19 (bottom left), 20 (bottom background) Bettmann/Corbis; page 6 (top right) The Granger Collection, NY; page 6 (bottom left) Phillip James Corwin/Corbis; page 6 (bottom right) Lake County Museum/Corbis; pages 6–7 (background), 23 (right), 27 (right) Corbis; page 7 (top left) Roger Garwood & Trish Ainslie/Corbis; page 7 (bottom left) Dave G. Houser/Corbis; page 7 (top right) Wolfgang Kaehler/Corbis; pages 8–9 courtesy Scotts Bluff National Monument; page 10 (bottom) Amon Carter Museum, Ft. Worth, Texas; pages 10 (bottom background), 28 (bottom) courtesy Library of Congress; page 11 (top left) MSCUA, University of Washington Libraries, NA3995; pages 12 (bottom inset), 18 (background) Lowell Georgia/Corbis; pages 12–13 Curt Teich Postcard Archives, Lake County (IL) Discovery Museum; page 13 (top right) Santa Barbara Mission; page 14 (top) National Archives; page 15 (right) from *Women's Diaries of the Westward Journey;* page 15 (bottom background) Craig Aurness/Corbis; page 16 Smithsonian American Art Museum, Washington, DC/Art Resource, NY; page 17 (bottom right) photolibrary/PictureQuest; page 20 (middle inset) James L. Amos/Corbis; page 21 (bottom background) Scott T. Smith/Corbis; page 22 (top) MSCUA, University of Washington Libraries, D. Kinsey 155A; page 23 (left) MSCUA, University of Washington Libraries, D. Kinsey A14; page 25 (right) Werner Forman/Art Resource, NY; page 26 (bottom background) Michael Maslan Historic Photographs/Corbis; page 27 (top left) Richard Cummins/Corbis; page 29 (right) Rykoff Collection/Corbis; page 30 (bottom) Joseph Sohm, ChromoSohm Inc./Corbis; page 31 (inset and background) The Kobal Collection/Picture Desk; page 32 The Oakland Museum, History Department, California.

Maps: pages 4, 15, 21 Sue Carlson

Produced through the worldwide resources of the National Geographic Society, John M. Fahey, Jr., President and Chief Executive Officer; Gilbert M. Grosvenor, Chairman of the Board; Nina D. Hoffman, Executive Vice President and President, Books and Education Publishing Group.

Prepared by National Geographic School Publishing

Ericka Markman, Senior Vice President and President, Children's Books and Education Publishing Group; Steve Mico, Vice President, Editorial Director; Marianne Hiland, Editorial Manager; Jim Hiscott, Design Manager; Kristin Hanneman, Illustrations Manager; Matt Wascavage, Manager of Publishing Services; Sean Philpotts, Production Manager; Jane Ponton, Production Artist.

Manufacturing and Quality Management

Christopher A. Liedel, Chief Financial Officer; Phillip L. Schlosser, Director; Clifton M. Brown III, Manager.

Program Development

Gare Thompson Associates, Inc.

Book Development

Thomas Nieman, Inc.

Consultant/Reviewer

Dr. Margit E. McGuire, School of Education, Seattle University, Seattle, Washington

Book Design

Steven Curtis Design, Inc.

Published by the National Geographic Society
1145 17th Street, N.W.
Washington, D.C. 20036-4688

ISBN 978-0-7922-8617-2
ISBN 0-7922-8617-0

4 5 6 7 8 9 10 20 19 18 17 16 15
Printed in the U.S.A.

Table of Contents

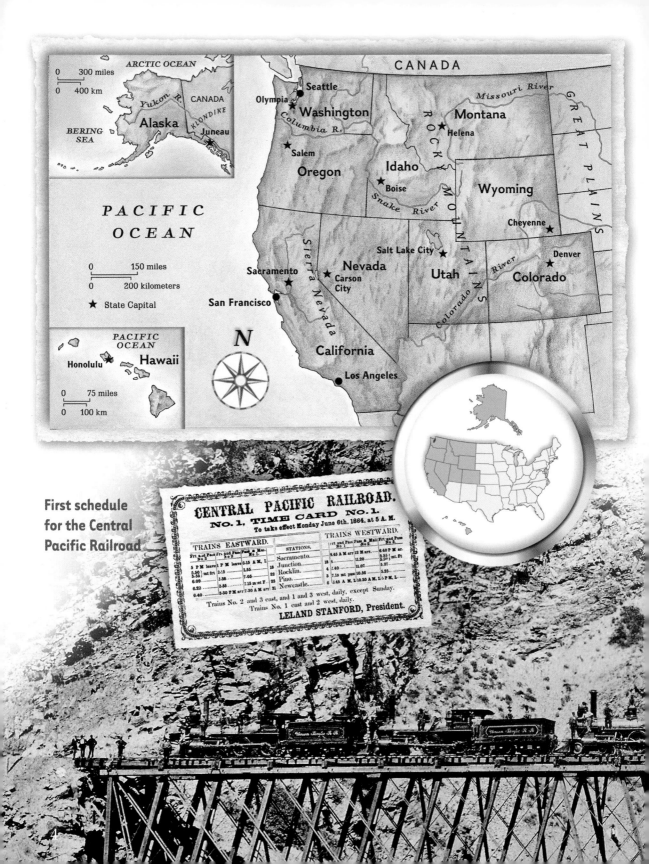

First schedule for the Central Pacific Railroad

CENTRAL PACIFIC RAILROAD.

NO. 1, TIME CARD NO. 1.

To take effect Monday June 6th, 1864, at 5 A. M.

TRAINS EASTWARD.			STATIONS.		TRAINS WESTWARD.	
Frt and Pass Frt and Pass Pass & Mail					Frt and Pass Frt & Mail Frt and Pass	
No 3	No 2	No 1			No 1	No 2
5 P M leave	P M leave	5.15 A M L	Sacramento	18	9.45 A M arr	12 M arr	6.40 P M arr
5.40 mt frt	2.15	5.55	Junction	13	4	.40	11.20	5.37
6.09	2.38	7.05	Rocklin	22	7.40	11.07	5.25
6.22	2.55	7.15 m wt F	Pino	25	7.19 mt pas	10.56	
6.40	3.30 P M arr	7.30 A M arr	Newcastle	31	6	3.45 A M, L	10.30 A M, L	5 P M, L

Trains No. 2 and 3 east, and 1 and 3 west, daily, except Sunday.

Trains No. 1 east and 2 west, daily.

LELAND STANFORD, President.

4

Introduction

Meet Your Guide to the West

Hi, my name is Ben. I come from America's "golden West." I would like to be your guide to the history of this wonderful region. The West is special for some big reasons.

To start with, it's so big and wild! The West has grasslands, forests, mountains, deserts, and seacoasts. Tourists come from all over the world to enjoy our wilderness areas.

Second, the West has so many **natural resources.** Our farmers grow much of the nation's food.

Our coastal waters are full of fish. Loggers harvest the trees in our forests. There's mineral wealth too—gold, silver, copper, and oil.

Last, the West is America's gateway to the Pacific region and Asia. The West has many large port cities, and these cities trade with cities in Asia. Many people from Asia have settled here.

That is what the West is like today. But what was it like long ago? Let's visit the West in the past to discover how it got this way.

Railroads were very important in the settlement of the West.

Time Line
of the West

The West has an exciting history. Here are some key events from its past. I'll tell you more about many of them as we go along.

1820s–1830s
Era of the
Mountain Men

1700 •••• **1800** ••• **1810** ••• **1820** ••• **1830** ••• **1840** ••••

1775–1783
American Revolution

1846–1848
Mexican-American War

1769
First Spanish
mission founded.

1842
Oregon Trail
opened.

1847
Mormons under
Brigham Young
found
Salt Lake City.

1848
California Gold Rush begins.

1869
Transcontinental railroad completed.

1850 • • • 1860 • • • 1870 • • • 1880 • • • 1890 • • • 1900 • • • 1910 • • •

▲
1861–1865
Civil War

1867
Alaska bought from Russia.

1898
Hawaii annexed.

1911
First Hollywood studio built.

1 Into the Wilderness

In the 1800s, Americans saw the West as a region where they could get ahead. There was rich land to farm here. There were forests for timber. There was gold and silver.

For thousands of years, many different Native American peoples had lived in the West.

In what are now Oregon and Washington, Native American peoples lived well by fishing and trading.

To the south was California, which had been a **colony** of Spain since the 1500s. In the late 1700s, the Spanish began building a chain of missions along the coast.

A **Spanish mission** was a settlement that included a church, living quarters, and farmlands. There was usually a nearby town where troops were stationed to protect the mission. The missions helped establish the Spanish way of life in early California.

In the early 1840s, thousands of people traveled west along the **overland trails.** These were taken by settlers going to the Oregon Country, Utah, and California.

For those who survived thirst, hunger, sickness, accidents, and other dangers, the trip could last six months. As people said then, "The cowards never started, and the weak died along the way."

Let's take a look at some important events in the early history of the West. First, we're off to the Northwest coast to see a Native American village.

Settlers moving west on one of the overland trails

A Chinook Village, 1780

Well, here we are on the Columbia River near the Pacific coast. It's raining, as it often is here. Dense evergreen forests stand on both sides of the river. Cloud-covered mountains rise to the east. Native Americans speaking the **Chinook** language live here. This land is rich with fish and furs and timber. The Chinook are great canoe builders, fishers, and traders.

The Chinook live in long houses made of planks from the cedar tree. Let's step inside. Many families live together.

They share an open area in the center around the fire pit. The hole in the roof above lets out the smoke. See the spaces along the walls? They're for sleeping and storage.

A Chinook house

Chinooks meeting the explorers Lewis and Clark in 1805

10

Look around. You'll see lots of things made from cedar. Cedar bark is used to make waterproof dresses, capes, and hats. The Chinook sleep on cedar mats and store food in cedar baskets. They also carve cedar into beautiful objects.

The Chinook gather oysters, crabs, mussels, and other shellfish from the sea. They also catch salmon from the rivers. They dry the salmon on rocks or smoke the fish on racks over the fire pit. Chinook women gather nuts, roots, and berries to feed their families.

But don't get too comfortable in here. We're off to California to visit a Spanish mission.

VOICES OF THE WEST

A Chinook Tale

"Once there was a boy who was lost and lived for years in the sea with the seals. After he was found, his parents taught him to walk, talk, and eat like a human again. But he longed to return to the sea. He was happy only when he carved beautiful things. One day at sea, he jumped out of his parents' canoe. They sadly dropped his carving tools into the water. But each spring, he floated a beautiful carving to them."

11

Mission San José, 1810

Welcome to Mission San José. We're just southeast of California's San Francisco Bay. It's a hot June day outside. But it's cool inside the mission's thick **adobe** walls. The red tile roof gleams in the sun. Doves of all different colors have gathered on the roof. They look like bright, shining jewels. Bells ring to call the people to church. We can hear their voices lifted in song.

Mission San José was founded by Spanish priests and soldiers 13 years ago. One goal of the missions is to bring the local Native Americans to the Catholic faith. Another is to give them Spanish culture. Some of the Indians come willingly. Others are forced by the soldiers.

Native Americans live and work here. Everyone at the mission must follow strict rules. Those who disobey are punished. Some choose to leave.

◀ **Song book used by Spanish priests to teach Native Americans to sing hymns**

San José is one of a chain of 21 missions that the Spanish built near the California coast—from San Diego in the south to Sonoma in the north. These missions and the nearby forts that protect them are the centers of Spanish power in California. The missions are also centers of trade. The missions grow grain and raise livestock. They produce wine, olive oil, hides, cloth, and tallow, from which soap and candles are made.

Now let's go east to the Sierra Nevada mountains where American settlers struggle westward along the overland trails.

Mission San José

Father Junípero Serra

People of the West

The person who started the Spanish missions in California was Father Junípero Serra. He was born in Spain and came to Mexico to teach the Native Americans about Christianity. When Serra reached California in 1769, he was more than 50 years old and in poor health. But in the last 15 years of his life, he founded 9 missions. Serra also brought Mexican cattle, sheep, fruits, and grains to California.

The crowded inside of a covered wagon

On the California Trail, 1850s

We're with a **wagon train** of settlers in the desert in what is now western Nevada. The glare of the sun is fierce. Distant mountains shimmer in the heat haze. This group of settlers is traveling on the California Trail. By now, they have come more than 1,200 miles from their starting point at Independence, Missouri. But they still have 800 miles to go before they reach California.

Settlers moving west endure many hardships and dangers. These include hunger, thirst, sickness, bad weather, rough country, accidents, and Indian attacks. The trails are lined with the graves of those who died along the way. Why do Americans go west? For many, it's the desire for land. For others, it's the lure of riches. Americans also feel it is their nation's destiny to expand to the Pacific Ocean.

Right now, they face many dry miles of desert. The settlers must move carefully. If a wagon breaks down or an ox gets hurt, it could be big trouble. But their biggest worry is water. At the last river, they filled up anything that would hold water. Will it be enough to get them across the desert?

Next the mountains must be crossed. Will the settlers make it over the mountains before snow falls and blocks the passes? Snow begins falling in October. Let's cross the mountains ourselves and see what happens when gold is discovered in California.

Amelia Stewart Knight

People of the West

In 1853, Amelia Stewart Knight traveled west from Iowa to the Oregon Territory with her husband and seven children. In addition to the other problems faced by all migrants, she was pregnant during the trip. Her eighth child was born in Oregon. Right after the birth, Knight and her family spent three days getting themselves and their belongings across the Columbia River.

Desert along the California Trail

Miners looking for gold in the mountains

Bonanza

In 1848, few people lived in California. But then gold was discovered here. Word of the discovery spread around the world like wildfire. Thousands flocked to California in search of gold. Few people got rich, but many stayed—enough for California to become a state in 1850. In 1859, there was an even bigger strike—silver this time—in Nevada. And there were others. Dreams of instant riches kept luring people to the West.

The overland trails were far too slow for this growing region. A railroad was needed to link the West with the rest of the country. In 1869, the first **transcontinental railroad** was completed. Other lines soon followed. With these railroads linking the West to the rest of the country, people and goods could move quickly and cheaply. Western towns grew into cities.

A growing West needed lots of wood for all kinds of uses, from building houses to putting out newspapers. The big forests of the East had been mostly cut down. So the loggers moved to the Pacific Northwest. By the late 1880s, logging had become an important industry here. It employed many workers.

Let's see how people used the rich natural resources found in the West. First, we'll join some of thousands who came to California looking for gold.

A gold nugget

California Gold Rush, 1849

We're here by the American River in California. There are over 2,000 men who have raced here looking for gold. They have been at it since the sun rose. Panning for gold is slow. The men take metal pans to the river to sift for gold. Gold is heavier than the river sand. As the men shake their pans, water and sand run out while the heavier gold stays. The men find very few nuggets.

Mostly they find gold dust. But still the hope of sudden wealth drives them, and they keep panning.

Life in a mining camp is rough. Most men sleep in tents. The tents often fall apart in the rain. There is no time for baths and not much to eat. Tempers are short, and few men trust each other. You hear them fighting over claims.

The American River in California, where gold was found in 1848

▲ A miner panning for gold

Everyone wants to strike it rich, but it seems like few do. As you listen to the miners working, you hear that many have left everything behind. Some just walked out of their jobs and came here. Others have left their families behind.

The local stores charge high prices for food. Miners spend most of the gold that they find. A bag of sugar costs about five dollars. A shovel costs fifteen dollars. Men buy some dinner and they are broke. Tomorrow they start over panning for more gold. As night settles, the men fall asleep, bone-tired, but still dreaming of riches.

Those who could afford it went to California by sea.

Over the years, more and more people came to the West. They needed a faster, safer way to get here. Let's leave the miners behind to go to Utah, where the first transcontinental railroad is being completed. All aboard!

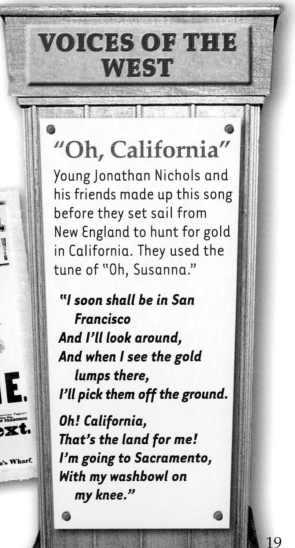

VOICES OF THE WEST

"Oh, California"

Young Jonathan Nichols and his friends made up this song before they set sail from New England to hunt for gold in California. They used the tune of "Oh, Susanna."

*"I soon shall be in San
    Francisco
And I'll look around,
And when I see the gold
    lumps there,
I'll pick them off the ground.*

*Oh! California,
That's the land for me!
I'm going to Sacramento,
With my washbowl on
    my knee."*

Transcontinental Railroad, 1869

Here we are at Promontory, Utah, on May 10, 1869. This is a very special day. Today, the Central Pacific Railroad and the Union Pacific Railroad will meet, linking the East and West coasts of the United States. The Central Pacific began laying track eastward from Sacramento, California, in January 1863. In July 1865, the Union Pacific started laying track westward from Omaha, Nebraska. Today, the two lines will be joined. Let's watch the big event.

Guests get out of private railroad cars, and a band plays. A group of Chinese workers from the Central Pacific and an Irish crew from the Union Pacific lay down the last track. Everyone cheers as California Governor Leland Stanford raises a sledgehammer to drive the golden spike created for this event. Oops, he misses. Finally, the spike is driven into the track! The two railroads are now linked.

▼ Workers from the Union Pacific and Central Pacific celebrating completion of the transcontinental railroad

◄ Golden spike used at ceremony marking completion of the railroad

The Central and Union Pacific trains on the track inch forward until they touch. Speeches are made and then food is served.

As dusk falls, the two trains back away from each other. Tonight, there is a dance, a parade, and more food, but we have to leave. We're off to a logging camp in the Pacific Northwest. Let's go.

Transcontinental Railroad

Land near Promontory, Utah

VOICES OF THE WEST

Bret Harte

Western writer Bret Harte wrote a poem about the Union Pacific and Central Pacific meeting at Promontory. A "pilot" is the front part of an engine, also called a "cowcatcher."

*"What was it the engines said,
   said,
Pilots touching, head
   to head,
Facing on the single
   track,
Half a world behind
   each back?"*

Loggers in a bunkhouse

Logging Camp, 1883

It is cool and quiet here in this forest in the Pacific Northwest. The tall trees tower above us. Let's walk to the logging camp. It's down that hill. As we get closer to the camp, we can hear the men talking. The loggers live in a big bunkhouse. The smell of breakfast hits us as we get closer to the cabin. The cook cleans up as the men get ready to leave the camp.

Logging is hard and dangerous work. The men gather up their saws and axes and set off for work. The trees here are very hard to cut down because they are so big. The loggers select a tree and cut notches in the trunk six feet off the ground. Then they shove planks into the notches. The men get on the planks with their saws. They use axes to make the front cut. Then they use saws to make the back cut. The tree will fall toward the front cut.

The men jump out of the way. They call the falling branches "widow-makers." Once the tree is down, the men strip the branches.

Some loggers have set up a road of greased logs. A team of oxen drags the newly cut trees along this road. This is the easiest way to get the trees to the railroad car. The railroad car will bring them to the sawmill.

The men keep working until the sun begins to set. It's time for us to leave too.

As time passed, settlers spread throughout the West. Let's see where Americans looked for new lands then.

Three loggers cutting down a huge fir tree

John Muir

People of the West

John Muir loved the wilderness. He spent years wandering alone thousands of miles on foot through the untouched mountains and forests of the West. Muir worked to save the American wilderness. In 1890, he helped establish California's Yosemite Valley as a national park. Two years later, Muir became president of the newly formed Sierra Club. Its goal was to preserve the wilderness.

Gold prospectors in Alaska

Pacific Empire

3

As the frontier areas in the West began to fill up, Americans started to look beyond their borders for new lands to settle.

Americans first looked north to Alaska, which was a Russian colony at the time. In 1867, the United States bought Alaska from Russia. Many Americans thought buying a land of ice and snow was a "folly." Few expected to find the vast riches that were later discovered in Alaska.

The United States then looked west across the Pacific to Hawaii. These islands were a kingdom. Few outsiders came here until the 1820s, when American missionaries arrived. By the 1870s, the Americans in Hawaii had become rich and powerful. In 1893, they helped force out the ruling queen. Five years later, Hawaii became part of the United States.

Come to Alaska and Hawaii and see what life here was like long ago. First, we'll go to Alaska on the day that it becomes part of the United States. Put on your warm clothes, and let's head north.

Statues at a temple in Hawaii

Alaska Territory, 1867

We're in Sitka, a small town in Alaska Territory, in 1867. Long before, the Russians had come here and built a fort. They traded for furs with the Native Americans who lived here. Alaska became a Russian colony of Alaska. Earlier this year, U.S. Secretary of State William Seward arranged to buy the region from the Russians for seven million two hundred thousand dollars. Alaska is a great bargain—about two cents per acre. But many Americans think it's a waste of money. They call Alaska "Seward's Folly" and "Seward's Icebox."

Today, October 18, 1867, is a special day. Russia turns over Alaska to the United States. People crowd Sitka's muddy street. American soldiers face Russian ones. Leaders make speeches. Papers are signed. Cannons are fired. A wind whips through the crowd, and people pull their coats tighter. Finally, the flag of the United States is raised. People cheer. Alaska is now part of the United States.

U.S. check to Russia for Alaska

Early Sitka

26

THE WHITE PASS CHRONICLE

GROWING WITH THE LAST GREAT FRONTIER

NEWS FROM THE KLONDIKE.
GOLD! GOLD! GOLD! GOLD!
Special Tug Chartered To Get The News.

The Land Of Gold

People of the West

Jack London

The American writer Jack London lived for a time in Alaska. In 1897, he joined the Klondike gold rush here. He didn't find much gold, but he used what he learned to write exciting stories about life in this new frontier. Among these are "To Build a Fire," *The Call of the Wild*, and *White Fang*.

What really put Alaska on the map, though, was gold. In 1896, gold was discovered in the **Klondike,** a district in Canada's Yukon Territory, which borders Alaska. From 1897 to 1899, nearly 100,000 people traveled through Alaska on their way to the Klondike. Later gold strikes in Alaska itself drew settlers, who set up fish canning, logging, and mining businesses.

But now we're off to Hawaii. So shed those warm coats and let's go!

Hawaii, 1893

Now we're in Hawaii in January 1893. Unlike other parts of the West, this land is made of many small islands. Volcanoes formed the islands thousands of years ago.

For a long time, Hawaii was a kingdom. At first, the Hawaiians had little contact with Americans.

Only a few merchants and whalers stopped here. In the 1820s, American missionaries came to the islands to convert the Hawaiians to Christianity.

Ceremony at Hawaii's royal palace when the islands become part of the United States

The families of these missionaries stayed on, becoming wealthy landowners and merchants. By the 1870s, these Americans were very powerful. They wanted to overthrow the Hawaiian ruling family and make the islands part of the United States. When Queen Liliuokalani came to the throne in 1891, she tried to restore power to the native Hawaiians.

Early in 1893, the Americans decide to act. On January 17, with the help of U.S. troops, they take over government buildings and declare that Hawaii is no longer a kingdom. To prevent bloodshed, the queen orders her subjects not to fight the Americans.

Liliuokalani herself does not give up. She pleads for her kingdom. But the Americans declare that the islands are a new country. Sanford Dole, an American born in Hawaii, is made president. The queen is forbidden to leave her palace. In 1900, Hawaii becomes a territory of the United States. Dole becomes its first governor.

Plantation workers came to Hawaii from China, Japan, Korea, and the Philippines. Over the years, the islands become a "melting pot of the Pacific." Well, that's our trip through the history of the West. Hope you enjoyed it.

People of the West

Queen Liliuokalani was Hawaii's first—and last—queen. She also wrote over 150 songs and a history of Hawaii. When she died, she left money to take care of orphans in Hawaii. The Queen Liliuokalani Children's Center still helps young Hawaiians today.

We've been to many different times in the history of the West and met many different people. We've seen how a vast wilderness was first settled. We've seen how the West's natural resources attracted settlers and how the region was linked to the rest of the United States by the railroad. We've also seen how Americans began to look beyond our borders for new lands—Alaska and Hawaii.

The West's beautiful wilderness areas continue to attract visitors from all over the world. People come to enjoy our natural wonders.

Old Faithful geyser at Yellowstone National Park in Wyoming

The West is still a region rich with natural resources. Our farmers produce great harvests of fruits and vegetables. Gold and silver are still mined here. But now big machines do the work instead of miners with pans. Oil is now one of the most important resources found in Alaska. Loggers still work in the Pacific Northwest. Machines do much of the work in this industry too.

The West is still America's gateway to the Pacific and Asia's gateway to the United States. The West is home to many Americans of Asian descent.

To understand the West today, it helps to know about life here long ago. Come back and visit us soon!

Then & Now

Hollywood

Filmmakers first came to Hollywood around 1910 because the sunny climate gave them more days to shoot outdoors. Here's what filmmaking looked like in Hollywood's early days and what it looks like today.

Glossary

adobe sunbaked mud brick

Chinook a Native American people of the Pacific Northwest

colony a territory ruled by a foreign government

Klondike a district in Canada's Yukon territory, which borders Alaska

natural resource something found in nature that is a source of wealth to a region

overland trail a land route taken by settlers from the east going west to the Oregon Country, Utah, or California

Spanish mission a settlement that included a church, living quarters, and farmlands

transcontinental railroad railroad linking the Eastern United States with the West Coast

wagon train a line of wagons traveling cross-country